CREDITS:

Cover Design	Fritz Colinet
Author Photo	Anthony Batista
Editor	Elizabeth Young
Graphic Design/Layout	Fritz Colinet at Retna Media

D1379684

"People who give you their loyalty, honesty and integrity, give them the world.

- Author Unknown

Writing this gratitude book has been such a therapeutic process for me.

I hope this exercise in gratitude will help you to explore things you are grateful for in your own life. You can read one exercise a day or just randomly turn to a page and allow the thought to guide your day. It's a way to plant a seed of awareness as you flow through each day.

Use this book as a guide to start your own daily gratitude journal. I have shared only 100 thoughts here about gratitude, and I'm sure there are millions more you can think of. Just let the gratitude of life's journey flow through you.

- D'angelo Thompson

D'ANGELO THOMPSON

1

I am grateful for all blessings,
seen and unseen.

Be conscious of what you are doing, thinking
and attracting into your life.

Consciously focus on vibrating on the highest
level possible. That means
constantly combating negativity and not just
receiving but sharing divine
interactions.

2

I am grateful and worthy
of happiness.

You and all souls in this realm are
worthy of happiness, dreams and
feeling safe.

Happiness is pure when you also wish it for
others, no matter their religion,
culture, nationality or
sexual orientation.

3

I am grateful to see beyond my present circumstances.

All things are temporary, no matter the length of time.

Enjoy this present moment
and give 200% of yourself to it.

If you can't be fully present,
then remove yourself, take a nap and
reboot your energy. I'm a huge advocate of
30–45 minute power naps, they can change
your whole perspective on an issue or decision.

4

I am grateful to be a faith walker.

Faith is such a strong word, and we are always being tested.

When the tests come, buckle down, do the work and open your eyes and heart for the answers.

I promise you, you will weather any storm. You were molded from a sacred, powerful, infinite and intelligent consciousness.

5

I am grateful that I see humanity in all things. Today I will be a blessing to many.

You never know what direct, loving eye contact or a kind word can do. It can be a bolt of energy or connection that another person needed for the day.

Be a blessing in the lives of others. Sometimes it's holding up the mirror so they can see a better reflection of themselves. Other times it's just being a light, a shoulder to lean or cry on and/or an ear to listen.

6

I am grateful that God's light is my navigating force today and every day.

Remember, every day you have an inner compass. You can tap into this compass through prayer, meditation and/or speaking your intention for the day.

There is a divine force always present and guiding you, let us never forget this even in the darkest of moments.

7

I am grateful that I will no longer chase anything or anyone.

Recently a friend advised me to not chase relationships, mainly friendships. I smiled and said that person died years ago.

What I meant by that was, I am keenly aware that like attracts like. If you come from a sincere place, you will attract exactly what you need in your life or repel it.

8

I am grateful that my branches stretch far and wide.

Just imagine, you/we are all a part of a divine tree of life. Some of us are the tree's fruit in various stages of development. Some of us are the tree's branches, which hold the fruit up to allow it to grow to its fullest potential.

A question of purpose lies in this metaphor. How are you a branch in the life of others? Do you nourish them with all they need to grow? Support them to avoid decay from disease, dramas/traumas? Help them to live to a ripe age and fulfill their chosen paths?

Is it for us to answer?

9

I am grateful my roots run deep.

From the very beginning, as a seedling in
the tree of life, our own tree(s) are allowed to
sprout and gain momentum.

The key is to make sure we are planted solidly
and to remember the "mother tree" is part of
our grand design. Our sacred DNA runs deeper
than any root.

10

I am grateful for the beauty and wisdom, gifted to me by sacred teachers, that is within me.

You are the pure essence of beauty and that reservoir flows from the inside out.

Some call it wisdom, some call it growth. You are simply beauty and knowledge in its purest form.

Receive, digest and share the wisdom from those who impart it into your vessel.

11

Today I am the miracle.

Breathe in and say, "I am a miracle. I am part of a divine, intelligent system of pure creativity. I will share my light with others."

Today I am the miracle.

12

I am grateful to accept all the lessons the universe has given me. May I use them to propel me into a new reality.

We are vessels forever downloading information.

We are powerful when we are centered in awareness of lessons given to us,
individually and or collectively.

Use these lessons to grow and step up to the challenges of life.

13

I am grateful for God's grace in my life.

Grace is such a beautiful word. It means simple elegance but in spiritual terms, Grace is the free and unmerited favor or God.

Let GRACE be the modus operandi throughout your life and daily interactions.

14

I am grateful that the truth
always reveals itself.

Think about it: men and women have been accused of crimes
and imprisoned for decades. Later, through DNA evidence,
they are found not guilty.

Imagine being sentenced to life in prison and/or death, and
the only thing you have is truth within your genetic code.

Truth is like a baptism and can flow over us like a great deluge
when many wanted blood.

In our present-day world, we demonize many people before
all the facts are gathered and presented.

In honor of these wrongfully imprisoned men and women, sit
still for a moment and speak this clearly to the universe: may
the truth always set us free.

This is the Age of Transparency, and the truth can no longer
be bound.

Seek truth always.

15

I am grateful to know fear and to step into it, in doing so I am delivered.

Fear is a powerful force of energy, and it digs deep into the mind of men. It can wage wars, justify mass killings, end marriages, demonize other human beings because of skin color, religious beliefs or cultural traditions.

Fear is a plague that ravishes our planet. What if we stepped into fear and unraveled its chaos? We can be truly elevated as a species by unraveling these untruths that keep permeating in our global society.

Being delivered from fear based consciousness and into a vibration of LOVE.

16

I am grateful to travel and explore this vast world.

Travel is the best education. Through travel you can engulf yourself in many cultures, languages, environments and energies.

The key is to be open and understand that others may live differently than you are accustomed to, but they all seek to be loved and experience joy with their loved ones and neighbors as you do.

In some places in the world, the reverence for Mother Nature and for one's fellow man is deeply rooted in culture.

There's no better feeling than to observe and be a part of this. Some of these places are considered poor or third world. Yet the joy and simplicity of true kindness that I've witnessed has made me weep and crave that connection in my "first world" interactions.

Marianne Williamson simply stated, "Each of us has a unique part to play in the healing of the world."

17

I am grateful for a healing heart.

The human heart is phenomenal, not only physically but spiritually. It can realign itself after it's been battered, diseased and/or deeply, emotionally hurt.

In knowing this, I am in awe of our ability to heal and even mend a broken heart. Especially in moments when you can't breathe or think you can't see another day. Somehow with time, you feel whole again and ready to embrace the new.

18

I am grateful not to be ruled by any addictions.

Our carnal desires can be highly addictive. What we can be addicted to is the high from feeling a heightened connection, whether it's for five minutes or 30 minutes or hours, with another person or substance.

There are many emotional and personal triggers that feed this side of our addictive personalities.

Like anything, we have to remember who controls our thoughts and our bodies. We do. State today: I am present and high on life. No other substance will control my life's purpose.

That said, there are individuals genetically and chemically prone to addictions, which requires talking to a professional.

Use this statement as another tool to keep you aligned.

19

I am grateful to be a child of light; darkness will never rule my today or tomorrow.

Simply, be the light in all the interactions you want to see in the world.

When darkness comes toward you, your light and energy blinds it.

Darkness has no idea how and where to attack you.

Marianne Williamson shares one exercise: After you meditate in the morning, and you walk into your day, ask, "Love walk in before me, to the right of me, to the left of me, above me and below me." It's like a protective shield for all your interactions.

Believe me, it works.

20

I am grateful to be fully present.

Being fully present is something that is rare in our social media driven lives. Social media is drawing us closer to extinction as communicative beings.

Be purposeful and present in your daily interactions, eye contact and acknowledgment of others.

When you ask the Divine to be present in your life, honor it by doing the same. For instance, a parent says, "I had no idea my child was in crisis." If you put down your devices, personally check in

and have quality face time together with loved ones, you may see warning signs when they are in crisis. I have been guilty of this oversight. I have misjudged someone's action, because I didn't understand it was a cry for help.

Being present is being aware, or being "woke" in the urban dictionary, to the experiences happening all around you.

21

I am grateful for a forgiving heart.

As part of allowing our heart to heal, we must be in a constant state of forgiveness and not dwell on the pain.

By no means am I saying stay in an unhealthy or toxic relationship.

You can forgive, but do the work so you are not accepting or attracting substandard relationships.

22

I am grateful for the pain that has elevated me to a better place in my life.

Pain or pressure makes diamonds. I'm sure you have heard this a million times before, but how true it is.

Many years ago I felt overwhelmed and subsequently broke out with a bad case of shingles, which left me bedridden and on antivirals and narcotic painkillers for 10 days.

Those 10 days gave me time to reflect on how I was handling my personal and professional life. I laughed when I realized that in order to sit still and gain clarity, I had to get drastically sick.

Think about it. People who have lived through the most horrific experiences (i.e., strong, intelligent and beautiful women such as Malala Yousafzai, Oprah Winfrey and Somaly Mam, to name just a few) still find the capacity to empower and love others.

Use pain to grow into a powerful phoenix and elevate your reality and the reality of others in the process.

23

I am grateful that the words
"past aggressions"
do not rule my tomorrow.

We have already spoken about fear. Jump into fear, and DO NOT let it define your tomorrow.

I think the curse of abuse is that the abuser can leave their victim unable to see past the incidents of abuse.

If you walk forward, speak about it, and heal, then neither the shame nor the abuser has any more power. Shame is like spiritual blackmail. You are forever imprisoned if you allow IT to be your story.

Break free and own this day and your tomorrow.

24

I am grateful to be guided by light but also understand there is wisdom in darkness that must be experienced.

For sure, the answer is yes, darkness can be a teacher.

Experiencing dark moments in life help you avoid walking into bad situations again and again.

Once you experience the depths of the absence of light, your being purely will not and cannot sit by quietly and allow this disconnect to prevail.

25

I am grateful to smile.

Just the action of smiling is a quiet sense of knowing that this too shall pass, or I am where I am supposed to be.

So when you are feeling stressed or anxiety ridden, just smile and say, "This too shall pass."

26

I am grateful
that I am an emotional being.

Sometimes we think showing emotion is a weakness. I beg to differ.

It's healthy to express how you are feeling (in a mature way, of course). We have emotions and should use them. They can be effective in getting your point across.

Never apologize for being authentic or being simply human.

27

I am grateful
to be connected to spirit.

We are more than flesh and bone. We hold a
powerful light within this temple we call the
human body.

To be connected in mind, body and spirit is
truly divine. It is the holy trinity if you will.

When we feel disconnected, all three parts
are not aligned and getting centered requires
conscious action. Whether it's a morning
activation prayer/meditation or simply reading,
do something that sets the tone for your day.

You stand in power when you are
wholly (holy) connected.

28

I am grateful that spirit is energy, and it's eternal. There is never loss, just new form.

When people contemplate death, most think it's our final destination.

Just think of death as a passing of energy that is never lost. It's either connecting to a bigger energy field or taking on a new form.

You are reading this book because on some level you know and/or believe this to be true, or you have experienced it.

Call it God or the universe or goddess energy or quantum psychics, IT just is.

29

I am grateful for this day
and all the lessons yet to unfold.

A lesson awaits us each day. Sometimes it's
subtle reminder, such as a gentle whisper or a
stub of the toe on a piece of furniture, telling
you to slow down. On other occasions, it's a
glaring billboard.

I personally need the glaring billboard on most
occasions, but with time I've learned to listen to
the subtle reminders/nudges that God gives us.

30

I am grateful for all beauty that manifests
in my life through others, in this I see God.

Have you ever observed a happy child or a family
pet and saw just pure love in their eyes? If you have,
you know there's nothing greater than having this
deep connection with another being.

Sometimes we need to see our light reflected back to
us through others, in this we can also see God.

Truly, no man is an island unto himself. A
functioning and sustainable island must have a
fresh water source, infusion of light and hopefully, a
solid foundation.

May your circle of love (friends and family) be
this island.

31

I am grateful that love has no class status, gender or religion, it just is.

LOVE, does not give you points for being wealthy, poor, a certain gender, sexual preference, anointed or not, religious beliefs, etc. Love just is.

Many years ago I had a standing once-a week-appointment with a spiritual teacher. He gave great advice based on our studies and interpretations of the organization's leaders' teachings and the sacred text.

One day, I shared a challenging situation, and he stated, "If a certain celebrity can do it, so can you." FIRE shot from my eyes. I said, "Yes, she CAN do it with three nannies, four assistants and multiple chefs." My point was neither she nor I was closer to God because of our bank accounts. My desire was pure, and I'm sure her desire was pure, too.

At that moment, I realized that students were being tiered according to economic status. It sickened me because I knew for a fact, during my entire life of seeking "the divine," God invited all to come to him, and that is pure love.

Let your spiritual practice be love, and all else will align.

D'ANGELO THOMPSON

32

I am grateful there are no borders,
except for the ones we put up.

In the world, at the present moment, borders
are a huge topic. I implore you to know that
building walls, drives us further apart.

Allow yourself to be open, to learn and to
expand. It serves you and the world at the
highest level.

Our purpose in this life is to elevate ourselves
and hopefully, others in the process.

33

I am grateful to welcome growth and transformation.

Transformational growth can be very difficult and challenging on many levels.

It is like building a new being, a new consciousness at a molecular level. Once you feel that expansion, your consciousness feels like your muscles after a hard workout. It hurts, but you know the discomfort is well worth the reward.

Then the growth becomes easier, but you still have to set new milestones.

Remember, I talked about those nudges we get from the universe. Heed the call. Don't let that intuitive pull get to crisis mode where you have no other choice but to change or die.

34

I am grateful for knowing
the power of balance and self-care.

I think if your spirit is aligned, you can work
more effortlessly on the mind and
body alignment.

We can talk about higher consciousness until
we are blue in the face but taking care of
yourself is necessary as well.

Higher consciousness is about being the
embodiment of all three in full alignment (but
please don't push your diet, books or workouts
on anyone).

35

I am grateful for all
the lessons learned.

Sometimes in life we are conscious and or
unconscious to what's going on around us.

Great lessons are learned and given in both moments.

Thank the creator for all lessons seen and unseen.

36

I am grateful that in moments of darkness,
I never lose sight of light.

We must all weather storms in our lives, and we
must remember that "the light" is always present.

It's up to us to evoke the light to protect and
guide us out of the darkest of night. The dark of
night can be an abusive relationship, a tyrannical
boss, stress, fear, disloyal friendships, anxiety,
loss, death, depression and so much more.

In all aforementioned moments or stages, speak
to and command the power of all that is good to
work miracles in your life or situation. Have faith.

Evoke this prayer for yourself as well as for others.

I am grateful to plant the seeds of awareness in the hearts of others.

We can only lead by example and being very aware in life is key to this.

Never lose sight of the world around you.

Share what you have learned, engage, discuss, debate but don't get caught up in dogma or boxes.

We want to invite and engage in a heightened sense of awareness.

38

I am grateful for all
the different tribes of mankind.

We live in a very diverse world of people, let us call them tribes. I wouldn't change that diversity for anything. It's truly what makes the world beautiful.

All the tribes is what makes earth an amazing classroom to learn, grow and create from.

39

I am grateful to know peace
even in times of war on the human spirit.

Be grateful and pray in times of peace but
also be grateful and pray in times of war. Two
diverse energies remind us to be strong, kind,
forgiving and loving of one another.

This not only applies to different nations but
within your family, toward your neighbors, city,
state, country and even on a global scale.

40

I am grateful to speak my dreams
into reality with fierce clarity.

Be a dreamer but also be very clear when you
speak about your dreams. Words are a powerful
force. They can plant a firm flow of energy into
making your dream a reality.

Speak clearly, move proactively and allow the
universe to do the rest.

Your job is to have the awareness and wisdom to
say YES, when the manifestation of your dreams
are presented to you.

41

I am grateful for each moment
that I am part of creation.

You are creation.

You are created.

You are creative.

In every nanosecond,
you are a conscious ball of creative energy.

Now go and build your empire,
whatever that means to you.

42

I am grateful to be inspired by the musings of other souls.

Throughout history men, women and children have been inspired by something or someone.

Creation is our muse.

God is our muse.

The universe is our muse.

Nature is our muse.

Sound is our muse.

Color is our muse.

Poetry is our muse.

A child's laughter is our muse.

We are our muse…so be a muse.

43

I am grateful for the Exodus,
the Middle Passage and the migration of
many throughout world history that allows
me to be exactly where I am.

For centuries, the human condition has been
continuously tested, pushed, destroyed and
rebuilt. Somehow, we see these transgressions
and find a way to build a brighter day.

You are exactly where you are meant to be at this
very moment, and you have a powerful legion
of angels to guide you.

Just break the chains of life that bind you to your
present circumstances.

44

I am grateful to be
the embodiment of divine design.

You are beautifully and organically designed by an
infinite intelligent source. There are no accidents
or mistakes in your creation.

Nothing compares to your uniqueness and
divine essence.

Remember this when doubts wash over you:
There are no mistakes, just divine order.

45

I am grateful that no prison
of mortal men can contain my spirit.

In my lifetime, I have watched people imprison themselves through impoverished ideals or circumstances, lack of education, addictions, abusive relationships, and/or extreme religious beliefs that have no room for the "other."

I have always wondered what prevents any of us from finding a way out. This is not for me to answer, but this I know for sure: the spirit cannot be contained.

If you desire freedom, no bars can hold you back.

Think about the great Nelson Mandela, imprisoned for 27 years in a South African jail. He used that time to study and forgive his jailers. Therefore I ask, "Who was really imprisoned?"

His spirit was always free.

46

I am grateful to know that my own chaos can be rewritten into a story of miracles.

Sometimes, we can get comfortable in our own chaos and can't see the other side.

I bear witness, when everything and everyone in your life does not align with who you are and/or where you want to go, it's time to be still and realize what's next.

I know this is not easy. Cleansing or detoxing can be the beginning of achieving clarity.

You can rewrite your journey daily. It's never written by other people's perceptions and expectations of how you should live your life.

Start with knowing that you breathe in life, and you are the miracle.

You can make something masterful and beautiful from what seems to be pure chaos. Just think, this planet we thrive on was nothing more than uninhabitable molten rock, water until some seismic shifts of consciousness breathed life into it/her.

47

I am grateful for teachers/seers.

We call them teachers, seers, clairvoyants, intuitive empaths, the anointed and spirit guides.

I am grateful to be in the company of them all.

With one phrase or insight, they can change the trajectory of someone's life. That intuitive empath can be your own inner voice as well.

48

I am grateful for the miracle of life.

Every breath I take is a miracle.

Every moment my five senses are used is
a miracle.

Every step I take is a miracle.

Every new day I get to see and experience
life is a miracle.

My very being, as I know it, is a miracle.

49

I am grateful for the cycle of life
that returns each of us to an
all-encompassing consciousness.

As I'm writing this, an amazing soul,
Stephen Hawking, has transitioned. He
approached life, energy, space as he approached
science. He is now part of the ever-evolving
particles of light and energy.

Death is never an ending. It is a "continuum" of
what is possible.

50

I am grateful for all souls that choose to heal.

We can either dwell in a place of pain or choose another path.

The path to healing is not always easy but making the choice is.

Today I choose joy, and in this joy, I will be healed. I am ready for any challenges to come, knowing that they will help me crossover to a better consciousness.

51

I am grateful
to be naked in the eyes of spirit.

In the eyes of spirit I have no form, just pure energy.

The clothing, shoes and body I possess is just a temporary ornamentation.

What I have materially, and what I do professionally does not define me.

I am clothed in pure consciousness of what is possible.

52

I am grateful for the power
of music and its healing attributes.

Music in any form can make you laugh, cry and
elevate your soul.

My life is a song, and through music I am healed.

Be the healing song (psalm) in the life of others.

53

I am grateful for the power of YES.

Living in a space of yes can be even
more powerful.

Challenge yourself for 21 days and say yes to
things you wouldn't normally agree to and see
where it takes you.

Just try it.

54

I am also grateful for
the power of NO.

Just as yes can be powerful so are words: no; no, thank you; or no, I don't think so. You get my point.

When you have the disease to please, your YES is actually a NO. In saying no, you are taking your power back.

Be firm in what elevates you.

55

I am grateful to receive.

All the gifts of light that I have received,
I am so grateful.

Be open to receiving, allow life and blessings to
flow all around you.

Receiving is as equally important as giving.

56

I am grateful for my failures and successes.

Life is not always a yellow brick road paved with gold. Life happens, and there will be failures and successes.

Both contribute to who you are, and how you handle failures or successes is a true testament to your being.

If something goes awry, it doesn't mean the universe is not on your side. It just means there's a greater plan/lesson at work.

57

I am grateful for my guardian angels.

Your guardian angels are here to protect you in this realm, just trust.

Many spiritual teachings believe we are born with celestial, ancestral and earthly guardian angels. You could say that you are very protected by legions of angels.

Assert today that you are surrounded and protected by beings of light that only desire your highest good.

58

I am grateful to know that
the God essence flows through me.

This I know for sure, without a shadow of doubt, that my essence and connection to the Creator is strong.

I will move forward in all situations fully aware of this divine connection that reaches out to all I encounter.

My God essence is the perfume that can't be defined.

59

I am grateful for my ancestors.

We all have a story, a history.

Wherever that family beginning started, thank all who came before you, and the ones you call parents who were the vessel to bring you here.

We are a sum of many parts, and for that I am eternally grateful.

60

I am grateful for the things
I do not understand.

In life, some things you get, some things
you don't. That's why we are here to try to
understand the lessons forged in our honor.

The first step is surrendering and admitting, I
do not know.

The second step is to ask for knowledge
and guidance.

The third step is to discern and then download
all the gifts the Creator wants us to know.

D'ANGELO THOMPSON

61

I am grateful to be a force
of proactive change in life.

Be about it.

Be that force of proactive change.

Being a procrastinator does not serve me.

I embrace change in all aspects of my life and
ask the universe to use me.

62

I am grateful to not be bound by hate.

As men and women we think hating or disliking
someone puts them in their place.

Hate actually festers like an open sore, a boil or
a virus. It's meant to harm its host.

It puts you in a non-receptive,
disconnected place. The other person's blockage
is only temporary.

63

I am grateful to know love.

To know love is to know God.

Love shows through your speech, actions and your eyes/heart/soul.

Love also shows in your deeds not only to loved ones but to a perfect stranger or those who don't know how to receive it.

64

I am grateful for
the power of intuition.

Intuition is your best friend forEVER.

Intuition is your guardian angel speaking.

Intuition is God rolling his eyes saying listen,
I don't want you to experience this today.

Intuition is your self-aware identical twin.

65

I am grateful to not be ruled by
the desires of just the material world.

My material possessions do not define my
place in God's great universe.

I am part of a collective, as we all thrive,
so do I.

I am an ever-flowing vessel of abundance, and
there is enough for everyone.

66

I am grateful for the wealth
in all aspects of my life.

I am grateful for the wealth of great health.

I am grateful for the wealth of opportunities
that surround me.

I am grateful for the wealth of God's light ever
present in all my daily interactions even when I
am feeling out of alignment.

67

I am grateful for all souls that we encounter in this life who teach us invaluable lessons.

I know that every person/soul on some level is teaching me a greater lesson about love.

Every experience I have is invited,
and I can choose to grow from it.

We are all students, teachers and/or observers
in this life.

68

I am grateful for the moments of knowing.

The moments I feel the most connected are when I feel the strongest connection to the Divine.

In my purest form I am all-knowing. There is no uncertainty of any kind.

69

I am grateful for the musings of the heart.

I have many heart connections that tug at my soul and cannot be explained.

I am a muse and am inspired by many things. I am never without a flow of creativity.

The life force of creativity flows through me.

70

I am grateful for the source in all aspects of my life.

The source is ever-flowing, and I should never feel a void or lack.

The only time I feel lack is when I consciously disconnect from the source.

The source is always available and at my beckoning. It never leaves you. It's your eternal mother, your purest light in all things.

71

I am grateful to have a bountiful (full) life.

My life is full.

I am here to give to and receive from the life
of others.

You/we are never alone. The angels of
light want to elevate you in your moments
of profound sadness and moments of
unimaginable happiness.

72

I am grateful to understand
there is ebb and flow in life.

I know that life has ups and downs just as the
universe expands and contracts.

I am here to grow, and life's lessons are here
to assist in that expansion.

I am more than just my environment. I can
break out of any box that I am painted into.

73

I am grateful to have many ways
of expressing my divine energy through the
arts in film/television, painting, dance, music
and writing (fill in the blanks).

My gifts are how I express God's love in this realm.

I am a creator and divine energy flows through
me so that anything I produce is at its
highest vibration.

My work and life is meant to inspire and expand
all those who feel connected to it.

74

I am grateful for a new day to be alive, healthy and in my right mind.

I am fully alive and present in each moment.

Consciousness of my health is also part of being
in my right mind. I am fully in tune to reality,
and no darkness will be my guiding force.

When I feel overwhelmed, I will quiet myself
and be still.

As I sit in that stillness, I know for sure
answers will unfold.

75

I am grateful for children
that give us hope and a promise
of our own evolution.

New life invites hope to a generation.

New life teaches us that we can always begin
again and right our wrongs.

New life teaches us the art of love in the purest
way and teaches us to be our best self.

New life ushers out old ideas and breathes in
new ones.

76

I am grateful for beauty in all the ways it manifests.

Beauty comes in all forms and expressions.

Today I see the beauty in all things even if the world tells me otherwise.

Beauty manifests in all things that we touch and connect with.

77

I am grateful to see clearly
in this realm and beyond.

There are many levels of consciousness, and I
see clearly in all realms.

In this clarity, I fear nothing, my third eye
burns with a clear understanding.

I am here today to be a guide and to be guided.

78

I am grateful for the power of laughter.

To laugh is to see the comedy in life.

Today I choose to smile, giggle and laugh with the consciousness of a child.

I will not take myself or life so seriously.
All things will flow as they should.

79

I am grateful for all the guides
that have assisted me throughout my life.

We are fully connected to the other side as
children, but most of us are disconnected
when doubt or faithless consciousness
is introduced.

I am aware and grateful for all guides that have
intervened in my protection and successes.

I may not always see you or show my
gratitude, but today I say THANK YOU!

80

I am grateful for all stages of growth.

Sometimes my growth has been a challenge,
but the challenge is welcomed in hindsight.

I know now that all things happen for me
when I am ready.

I have no regrets at my current stage and will keep
planting and watering all seeds of opportunities.

81

I am grateful to BE.

Being is apart of my true state, and I never need to apologize.

May I always have a keen sense of awareness and live in a space of clarity.

Being does not just mean sitting still. It also means forward movement.

I am in a constant state of motion consciously and unconsciously.

82

I am grateful to not judge anyone's journey even though I may not understand it. Their journey is theirs to unlock.

In our society we are quick to judge what others should or should not be doing. How about sending them a burst of light/wind to propel their dreams forward?

To sit in judgment of anyone's journey, as many sacred teachings warn, you draw the sword of judgment on yourself.

Breathe blessings into the lives of others, that's all.

83

I am grateful to know that
our family or tribe are souls we have chosen
or that have chosen us.

Imagine that before you entered this realm
you knew the souls and experiences you
would encounter.

Our families, relationships or tribe are here to
teach us, assist us and elevate us in all that we
possibly can learn, be and do.

We are beings that are not always fully
conscious of our choices but somehow,
whichever road we decide to travel along, we
find our way.

84

I am grateful that life
is not always wrapped up
in a perfect package.

Life is not always wrapped in the perfect package.
Some of the most influential and profound
human souls didn't start out in ideal situations.

Be grateful for the perfections and
imperfections in life, all is a perfect recipe.

Every flower on a rose bush is not identical or
perfect, yet it's still a rose.

85

I am grateful for the gentle whispers,
when spirit (intuition) tells you ENOUGH,
it's time to make a move.

Intuition is masterful and one of the greatest
gifts the creator equipped all of us with.

When my gut says to move on or enough
already, I will heed its call to action for
forward movement.

In this shift guided by intuition, I know I will
always be okay.

86

I am grateful for the board game called LIFE.

In the game of "Life" or "Monopoly," you take risks in order to advance/grow.

You are here to master this board game for your specific desires and dreams. Sometimes we are slowed down to assist others along the way and in doing so, be present.

Pauses, potholes or detours are just a part of the great universal game called LIFE.

87

I am grateful to not be a pawn
in anyone's Shakespearean tragedies.
I am a seeker of truth and love only.

Shakespeare masterfully described the human experience through plays about love, jealousy, tragedies, dramas and madness.

Today I choose not to be cast in those plays, especially the madness of Lady Macbeth, drama of Hamlet and tragedy of Romeo and Juliet. Those are not characters I choose to play in life.

Even though I'm aware that this can be the human condition, it does not have to be my daily condition or digested in my DNA.

88

I am grateful for all business opportunities and partnerships.

Many people and experiences cross our line of vision in life.

I am grateful for all the flow in my life.

I am grateful for all blessings seen and unseen.

I live in a space of YES and with this clarity, I will manifest exactly what I need and more.

89

I am grateful to be a vessel
open to learning and growing.

Each day I learn, and I'm fully open.

My vessel is open for an overflow of lessons
and growth of the soul.

Today I invite all that is new to heighten my
awareness and fill my vessel with pure knowledge.

90

I am grateful to be a sexual being and fully aware of the sacredness of my body and spirit connection.

My body is sacred, and I will always respect it.

In respecting my body, I protect it from disease.

In understanding the mind, body and spirit connection, I seek only elevated sexual connections.

91

I am grateful to invite the light
into all my interactions.

When I awake, I invite in the light.

As I walk through my daily interactions,
I invite in the light.

As I travel throughout the world,
I invite in the light.

May I be the embodiment of light in all of
my interactions.

92

I am grateful to be the star,
supporting cast, guest star or featured extra
in many "Lifetime" movies.

Whatever role I am meant to play,
I will play it well.

In this movie called Life, I know we are cast in
different roles, may I accept them graciously.

My ego will not prevent me from playing the
BEST role of my life, may the Creator cast me
where I am needed to bring the most light.

93

I am grateful to know that when we reflect on conversations that we didn't value initially, we discover gems of wisdom in hindsight.

Have you ever recalled a conversation that you had with your parents years ago, and all of sudden, you realize their advice contained a seed of wisdom?

I embrace all gems of wisdom, even when I am unaware of them at the moment.

I know the universe sends us many guides. I just need to listen and be aware when precious stones of information are being shared for my higher good.

94

I am grateful for this planet that offers us a home to live on and prosper in.

Earth is my physical home.

I am grateful for all that she provides, and I will fight to protect her.

She nourishes my body and my global family with fresh air, food, water and nature in all its glorious forms.

I will share the prosperity she bestows upon us all in a bounty of ways.

Today I say thank you to Mother Earth.

95

I am grateful for my life.

May I always stay in a place of gratitude.

I am grateful for the form and body my soul is housed in.

I am forever morphing as life prepares each of us to be stronger versions of ourselves.

I am.

96

I am grateful for all who conspire
in the success and advancements of others.
I am grateful to understand the same blessings
flow into their lives as well.

I give with the consciousness of flow and
abundance in my life and the life of others.

For those who bless my coffers with an abundance
of opportunities, may they also be blessed.

We live in an abundant conscious realm that
wants us all to have what we need.

Today, I vibrate on the FLOW of prosperity.

97

I am grateful to give.

May I always be in a place to give not only
monetarily but of my time, advice,
home and friendship.

I give because I understand and download the
law of giving into my DNA.

In the act of giving, I am always blessed and
connected to the Creator.

98

I am grateful that I can see,
all veils are lifted.

May my eyes always see deeply.

May my ears always be discerning.

All veils are lifted. I will see into the infinite
and will always have pure clarity.

99

I am grateful to know the
power and laws of attraction.

I am built to be powerful.

I will attract all that I need and desire.

I am a whole and a pure being and well aware
that the universe wants me to be more than
just alright.

I will vibrate on being fully conscious in
my thoughts.

100

I am grateful to know that all beings
around the world are in the process
of being born, exploring, learning, loving,
growing, evolving and transitioning.

So, i ask you, "why resist"?

There is a flow, sometimes smooth and at other
times tumultuous but you always end up where
you're supposed to be. Sometimes detours
are needed.

Thank you all for taking this journey of gratitude with me. I am grateful for each of you and may this bring just a little more light and awareness into the world.

Special thanks to the people and thought processes that taught me gratitude at a very young age as well as my adult teachers: my mom (Ruth Lee Godbolt), Great Aunt "Peasie" Clara Alexander, Uncle Matthew Thompson, Bob Webber, the Holy Bible, The Artist's Way, The Seven Laws of Attraction, Kabbalah, the Zohar, *A Return to Love*, *A Course in Miracles*, Sonia Flotteron, Candice Harper,

Naomi Pabst, Julie Henderson, James Chambers, Marieme Djigo, Rodney Fitz-Hughes and Peter Georgotas.

This book is dedicated to the memory of
my best friend's mom,
Ms. Carmen America Arias.

ABOUT AUTHOR

D'angelo Thompson has worked in the creative arts industry close to three decades, which he cultivated while attending Pratt Institute in Brooklyn, NY.

Fashion, fine art, beauty, and writing has always been a passion. His earliest memory of writing was a poem he submitted to a local nature newspaper. The newspaper published the poem and was the creative push he needed to devour books, write, and read more.

Over the years he has published three beauty books (Enhanced Beauty, Enhanced Beauty for Teens, and Enhanced Beauty: Men's Grooming) that can be found through many retail outlets: Amazon, AuthorHouse, Barnes and Noble, Target and Walmart.

Throughout his life, he has studied many spiritual/religious thought processes and integrated many of these teachings into his everyday interactions. This book series is a way to share many of the sacred lessons, but mainly to emphasize the practice of gratitude.